and we were so far from the sea of course the hermit crabs were dead
___

Mitchell Reford

All rights reserved; no part of this book may be reproduced by any means without the publisher's permission.

ISBN: 978-1-913642-52-5

The author has asserted their right to be identified as the author of this Work in accordance with the Copyright, Designs and Patents Act 1988

Book designed by Aaron Kent

Edited by Aaron Kent

Broken Sleep Books (2021), Talgarreg, Wales

Contents

A Diaristic Quality but Everything is Still Gone	7
Last Summers	8
The First Time They Want You.	9
Foraging	10
Grass Seeds	11
Safe Sex	12
A Memory	13
SMALL-TOWN FUCK GEOMETRY	14
There have been many times food has been like…	15
BED-STUY YOU CAN'T EVER HAVE ME	16
Religious Art	17
Jonas Mekas at the Tate Modern	19
Sightseeing	21
Mice	22
Check Up	23
Today, I want to marry you.	26
Champs bar and cafe on a Tuesday night, and all the rest	27
All our sexts as necessary fictions	28
A poem for my IUD	30
Cat	32
Living through history	33
South for Winter	34
Acknowledgements	35

and we were so far from the sea of
course the hermit crabs were dead

Lotte Mitchell Reford

A Diaristic Quality but Everything is Still Gone
-- After Nan Goldin

A little sunsuck makes everything flutter. Everything hum.
The idea enters that once the world was a bit more sepia and makes it
safe. It seeps into all I have ever had, too. Redoes memories. Cracks
underfoot kill, so just jump. Friends are erudite and perpetually laughing.
Everyone is trying to fuck always and often succeeding or else sleeping
something off. When does a bare mattress look sexy? Only in a photograph.
Drinking while shitting also looks good, deified by this golden
hue. A big shining man is sucking his own dick. No one looks
at the camera; it's like it is still happening. The boys are young
and locked in softish battle or at least no one is hurt yet. Nothing
moves which means it is so damn full of lust. Pick out
what is signified - lips on a drag queen red as injury. Thin people
ignoring one another, presumably lovers. Wide lapels, Nike caps,
a punch just connecting with a cheekbone. It's like stock photos, but shot
only for me. The light on textured wallpaper through smoke,
smoke in every picture. I could write a sonnet just to smoking
in old photographs. To smoking in the bath or over dinner.
To smack and crack and pissed pants as they are retold
or remembered a little sunsucked a little sepia. All my lovers
sunsucked and sepia, all quietly sleeping, after the act
but before I leave. Greer is holding her wrist, testing its reedness,
testing the gaps, how much nothing she can hold around it.
How much she can be nothing. When people stopped smoking
in pubs they stank. All the vomit all the spills were real.
In the smoky mountains I once saw a dead wolf, really, a dead wolf
by the interstate. I remember it, a stock photo.
A great big fucking wolf wreathed in smoke. It couldn't get us,
it was dead. It was stuck just right there.

Last Summers

Before you think yourself grown you are spit and puddles of sun and sneaked cigarettes. You are dust from beneath anaemic grass. Your calves are marked by abandoned ring-pulls. You can't see your Gameboy Colour for the brightness of the sky so you learn how to jimmy open a car window and steal change from glove compartments. You spend the change on ten-pence sweets and Space Invaders. The sweets melt in your pockets. You eat them anyway. You are always sticky. You press your body against other skinny sticky bodies in stairwells still in off-brand shorts and T-shirts. You don't do more than press. You are wet but you don't think *I am wet*. When you unpress yourself from the neighbour girl you are playing-out with the two of you race to the balcony. This is your favourite game. You throw everything you can over the balcony's lip. Fruit, eggs, matchbox cars, water bombs. When the paving slabs dry the new-clean patches are grey in the brown. You sit on the edge of the balcony, and your shorts dig into surprise-fleshy thighs. She holds you and you think she will drop you and you think that she won't drop you. You go home when the sun has set. You pierce your own ears when everyone else is asleep and enjoy the way they ache in the morning because it is all you can think of. You flick matches into garbage bins and wait for the flames to warm your face. To reflect in the eyes of the neighbour girl, her blinks regular as the ticking of a clock.

The First Time They Want You.

You are at a funeral the first time a man tells you you've grown into
a fine young woman. Or does he say *Budding*? The man is old.
He is probably related to you but who knows, all old men look the same.
At dinner in the hotel, the meat looks like tongues and tastes like grass,
tastes like braces in someone else's mouth. It has been said recently, *Budding*,
and you can't stop thinking of the word of what might grow from it and from
you, of how last time the family was together like this,
you sat under the table with your cousins and ate and ate
and now you want to go outside and taste the night air,
you want to drink what your mother is drinking, the wine staining her teeth.
You touch the lamb on your plate – press a finger in
to watch the blood snake into your nail. You are laying on hands,
you will think the animal back to life, imagine it coming together at the table,
a surprised sheep wet from rebirth, wool matted. In the hotel room
You hang out of window smoking and your shoulders are cold
above your dress. You are so full of spit and blood and it is moving so fast
and you wonder about if this thing had been open casket,
if you had placed a hand over your grandmother's face and let it all rush
to your palms. You felt the men follow you like they follow food
their eyes yellow and hungry. They want to open dark mouths and take you in
want to stop your photosynthesis, but you have turned your face to the sky
to all the stars visible out here in the country. You blow smoke through chapped lips.
You know there are more stars than you can count; you know the longer you look
the more you will see. You wonder why you decided to look up.
You wonder why you would ever look away.

Foraging

I don't eat blackberries any more
                    not since I saw a crop of maggots crawl from inside
                the fruit   in a bowl

we had been out to pick them   alone

found untouched brambles   verge-side on a motorway
       the blackberries were big
and tight   like clusters of dark eggs   and left for a while
      out from them crawled these larvae   like   fingernail clippings
or   white rice
                in health class we watched
a film of birth   a bloody head emerging from between legs
       this mammalian image didn't bother me
but the video was in reverse   and soon   ovulation
began   a maze of hot red caves   and a cluster   of eggs
      like fruit on a bramble
this is what happens inside you once a month   the voiceover said
      as one bulb of berry   detached
and I screwed my eyes tight   stuck fingers
     in my ears   I thought I would never be ready
              for this kind of thing to happen to me
but our bodies have their own agendas

                    When finally I began   as promised
to cramp
        and bleed for the first time
        I was not surprised to find

        smashed blackberries in my underwear
                    juice staining my thighs.

Grass Seeds

The grass seeds get into my knee because there is a cut, closed with butterfly stitches. It is summer and the crickets are loud and nothing is ordinary. *This will scar*, my mother says, applying the butterfly stitches. Someone says, *you should go to A&E*. School is finished for summer. My leg is cut. I am in the grass, in the park, and the grasshoppers are loud. Summer is not ordinary. I kneel in the grass to catch bugs, and when I get up my knee is full of seeds. They are sitting in my flesh where the butterfly stitches have come unstuck. They look like unhatched eggs. Butterfly eggs? I can't help but look closer. Some kind of fear rises in me. My mother helps again, washes out my knee. I forget my bug collection project. Before school starts back, my knee heals but all that year I am afraid. I look at my knee closely whenever I can. I know something is in there, waiting. I know that if I am not careful something will burst from me and begin to blossom. Something will nose out of me, and it will never go away.

Safe Sex

I have a system where I ask them, *Are you a murderer?* and it's pretty solid
it's worked every time so far. Normally the boy will laugh and say,
Yes, I have an axe upstairs, or else he will roll his eyes, or I will think he is rolling his eyes
at me in the dark. I will want to put a hand over his face, lay my fingertips
over his eyelids and press the heel of my palm into his mouth. Instead usually I wait
and keep my fingers by my side. I let his hand move to mine like he's making
the decisions. Sometimes, though, when I ask, *Are you a murderer?* A boy
will look shocked. He will look so shocked I know he has never thought
about hurting anyone, about teeth digging into his skin and spit on his wrist.
He has never even thought of hurting himself, not even in passing,
not even a little bit, not even a pinch that ends in a twist not even a thumb
curled into an out-flooding bruise or a butter knife pressed into flesh until it turns
white as lard until it turns pink as *What the fuck am I doing* until blood
is drawn despite it being a butter knife. This boy, he has never even drunk
so much he bled all over his white shoes or he did it once and never again
or he at least threw the shoes away, didn't keep them like a trophy like a talisman,
like a lucky rabbit's foot. He didn't wear them at Halloween the next year
like, *Fuck you,* didn't vomit on them this time didn't sink them in mud
and late October mulch. And when a boy looks like that looks surprised
and then says, *No, God no, why would you ask that?* And maybe pulls
me to him in a one armed hug maybe puts his face in my hair,
I don't so much want to come upstairs with him and I have to find a way
to forget the surprise, to forget the story he told me earlier about fishing
with his father and the one about how they named three dogs the same
because his little brother didn't yet understand death and his mum wanted
it to stay that way so I ask him what his dog was called and he tells me
and it's something unimaginative and a while later, in the middle of things,
the things we were headed upstairs to do, I can't help myself I yell, *Call me Fido,*
and I make sure he feels my wet mouth all over him.

A Memory

here we are at a party and you're wearing
something stupid round your neck
a dinosaur on a chain maybe you tell
the worst story is it about sticking
your dick through the hole in a fussball table
where the ball is supposed to enter
play no matter it never mattered
I know from your laugh the way it ruins
your whole face and from your terrible
posture that I will love you and I am not wrong
I touch your fingers in your pocket
in the dark this is weeks later then
your semen on my arms at work dries
and flakes like I am shedding a skin ushering families
into the movie theatre and cleaning old popcorn
out of plush seats it is okay
the long winter when it snows
and love balloons and the space
it takes up surprises us both
until eventually it thins like rubber
the point of this now is not to rehash
or to ask anything new of then
just I found a plastic dinosaur recently
ten years after that first one hung
against your chest I picked it up
from the dirt thousands of miles from you
but it made me want
to ask how I do it again
how do I know and let something
expand surely I am too old
to hang around the edges
waiting for a laugh to fold me in two

SMALL-TOWN FUCK GEOMETRY

We start with this joke, that in any given room there's someone
one or both of us has fucked. This is almost true here

and at first we point them out, but our pointing fingers
get tired, so tired we feel headachey and a little jealous.

We stop pointing. We draw 'x's across our nipples, because they are treasure
 and you stab the lid of a mason jar,

we are going to save our coins for a move. I've got to get out
but I have no sense of direction. I blame Google Maps,

you blame poetry. You tell me I have both in my pocket, but only one helps us at all.
I am pouring myself everywhere but never fitting. I can't stay straight. It's cute in the bath

but not in the street. I guess I should have seen this coming.
When you take our savings to the bank they total

five dollars forty-five. Not even enough for a bottle
of brown liquor. The thing is, in any given room here there's someone

one or both of us have fucked, or will fuck. Isn't that funny?
Fucking other people. Imagine me fucking other people.

I know you do already. It's the geometry of this small town
and of the way you and I cross, perpendicular

when what we need is to be parallel, or maybe to intersect
at multiple points. If we knew anything about maths maybe

we would save more money, or I would be able to control
the angles at which I fall. But how things are - we're all just

lines, crossing at random on various planes. You always wanted me
to write poems about you, and I guess now I am. We end with this joke

that in any given room there is someone one or both of us has fucked, and you want that
to stop, and I can't stop it, and anyway, I think we might be in different rooms entirely.

There have been many times food has been like...

Once, a Turkish grandmother showed me how to smash the pit
of an apricot, after I had sucked the flesh from it,
and remove the almond inside. I was told
at her family's kitchen table every morning to eat more
but I didn't know what this meant, I said, *I'm full*,
but I didn't know what this meant either. I brought a stone down
on the pit between sticky fingertips and some part of me hoped to crush myself
and find my seed, my pulp. She said, *Eat, eat,* or she said it with her hands,
lifting them to her mouth waiting for me to follow the instruction
before she slipped the fruit's small white heart past her own lips.
Do you know how good food can taste? I have never
thought about sex half as much as I have about a slice of toast.
This is not supposed to be funny, but it is. I had a friend,
years later, who worked at a health food store
and told me that people were dying from the cyanide in apricot pits.
The right amount is supposed to cure cancer; the wrong amount will kill you.
When I walked circles around my city, on every bridge I thought
I would fall lighter than a thrown set of keys. Could float up and over
the railing even. This is the closest I have felt to gods: lying
awake with the memory of fruit and every healthy thing
around me sleeping peacefully. The way the bruises on my body from where
it touched itself were like a language, but no one I presented my skin to
could read them. I am not saying I would go back, I know starving is solid
rock painted to look like an apricot grove and I know I have swallowed
too many pits already, I am just saying
there have been many times hunger has been like
a cut tether.

BED-STUY YOU CAN'T EVER HAVE ME

We are eating crisps that she calls chips but really I guess
they're puffs. They orange our palms and the pads of our fingers
and the bed linen is so white we keep our hands elevated.
It is our first christmas and our first New York and we had beer
for breakfast. She asks me to write an ode to her tits
and I ask her if she has read much Keats because odes
tend to be sort of depressing, for the most part
and he did all the tubercular dying shit,
and O', I hope her tits won't haunt me, but still
I tell her I will write about her when we break up,
which is the kind of thing she hates me saying
but is the kind of thing I say all the time.
All I want really, is to eat and drink and fuck
and never argue, but apparently there is a future
out there somewhere and a now nearby and all
that means work and tears and pinching at myself.
On her iPad we watch 'The one where…'
we are in a studio in Bed-Stuy and if either
of us could do the splits our feet would touch
both walls. We all suspend disbelief for plenty.
She puts a finger in her mouth for the Cheeto dust,
her American teeth scraping the American flavor
powder onto her tongue, and on-screen
an out of work actor enters his Greenwich Village
apartment. Outside, the sky is a perfect December white,
and it is Christmas day and the streets are quiet
except for the Orthodox Jews who are not on holiday.
Inside, her skin is soft and warm and only a little stained
with Cheeto dust, and neither of us believe
in god or anything, neither of us likes Christmas,
so maybe today could be any day? And then,
her tits would never have to haunt me.

Religious Art

Two separate friends have shown
me The Ecstasy of St Teresa
recently. Their readings on Bernini differed,
one using two fingers
to zoom in on her face and the fold
of her robes
observing how, lost like that,
she represents the infinite
in as much as we can ever touch
the infinite; in dreams and in
stone made soft and in how long stone lasts.
The other pointed out that her perfect
spread toes are the perfect spread toes
of orgasm, which comparatively might
seem crass, but orgasm is also an attempt at
a few seconds of infinity, an attempt to more
than just exist. He says *I've always liked
this bit on a girl* with his lips
in the fold of my thigh
and I can feel the saints above us–
Basil with his fingers almost touching as if he has
something to say but can't quite find
the words, though maybe if we give him
enough time he'll deliver.

When we're done and back to our hangovers
the boy stands and looks for his pants,
says, *I like the icon paintings*.
I didn't put them up there to watch over me,
but now I suppose they have no choice
and I like how they remind me of better places
where even religion is beautiful,
steeped in blood and gold leaf.
Last night he told me
about his Baptist upbringing.
How he has only recently stopped being afraid
of everything. He told me about architecture;
how he likes circles, how he likes poured
concrete but also Borromini. He told me,
Architects love things that seem impossible
and I told him that actually sounds pretty
brave, and maybe that is where
infinity is hiding --

in the almost impossibleness of art.
For example in a poem,
when meaning blooms
in the crack of light between two lines
like moss on old rock,
or in the scalding blue of those monasteries
in Montenegro, where I dropped money into
an honesty box and sometimes palmed two
gold-haloed saints, and people walked in straight lines
down carpet worn flat and black
to kiss the forehead or toes of Jesus,
Mary and Joseph. He kisses my shins,
though we are far from religious reverie,
and on the wall above us St Basil remains stern in almost-prayer,
his palms never touching, the space between them
reminding me that no skin ever really touches any other skin,
that atoms are only ever almost pressed together
infinitely close but always apart.

Jonas Mekas at the Tate Modern

Someone has fallen asleep in the dark of the gallery;
their snoring reminds me that we all die horribly
and of the time you told me to look out the window at the moon,
the way I said, *the moon is boring.*

On screen the little iron fences in the parks are the same.
Wooly hats are the same.
The baby, like all babies, is covered in spit.
Snow is a nuisance, a joy, the same.
House plants are brown at the edges,
moving, a hassle,
pizza is just the same,
cars are maybe brighter,
striped T-shirts are striped T-shirts,
and the moon hangs in the sky.

It reminds me that we all die horribly and
of the time my father cried because he found a cat
mummified beneath the floorboards of the family room,
how you said *life is boring*
like you were spitting out three olive pits.

Coca cola signs are the same on shop-fronts
and trees are naked just the same.
There is more coal everywhere,

and if life is boring then what's the point?
Unless it's the way the camera drops suddenly
to catch something new
and the world becomes a quilt of colour.

How we all die horribly, and the night that I left you
I got that coffee from a petrol station on the M1,
when I was about to fall asleep at the wheel,
how perfectly a bite comes out of a Styrofoam cup,
a half-moon,

and there's the dirty feet of the the artist's daughter,
the Velvet Underground's first show,
in an apartment uptown, in front of a striped T-shirt that's
a striped T-shirt,
and the way bad dancing is the same, and
light falling in long squares down a hallway is also just the same.

There is Jonas Mekas at 90 still keeping these video diaries,
and there's the itch to leave the restaurant
to write a stupid poem.
There's the decision to stay and talk awhile
over stained napkins

and there's the times I've seen my father cry:
when he was sick, when his best friend jumped from a balcony,
sometimes when I leave.

There's the fact that he found the lost cat at last
and cradled it carefully and laid it on the rug
and called me and told me the story;
how some old heartbreak he had almost forgotten
had been waiting under our feet all along,
out of sight and still the same.

Sightseeing

We stand in the church outside the walls on
the hottest day of the holiday
and you look up and say, *I feel like she's bearing down on me*
though she floats metres above us and I know that
you are probably just weird about bones
and all these indoor graves
because no one you have ever known is dead.
She never bore down on anyone, I say,
that was her problem, and you say *very funny*,
where will we have lunch because you are always
hungry in Rome.

Don't worry, I tell you, *her skull isn't even here*
and *skull* is too much, so you sit and
your eyes are raised in suspicion which looks,
from up here, like piety.
Don't you think she's pretty? I ask, my thigh and hip
pressed against the cool marble of a column,
and you cease your religious reverie for a moment
and glance in my direction, taking in my
sweatpatches and stretched out dress
and you say, *I think you're pretty.*

then your eyes fly up again, as if this might offend poor Agnes,
who could do nothing about it anyway, hanging
up there caught in gold, and also piled
as dust fine as face-powder, in two separate boxes.
Her cheeks are a little chubby, you say, and I tell you
she was only thirteen or maybe twelve when she lost her head
so that isn't really fair, and you tell me that honestly, you are starving,
and stand and take my hand, and I feel for Agnes, missing
all of this

    as we walk

        towards the blinding white of the door and I pull you closer

thinking that you will know dead people eventually,
and one day we if we have a daughter you might slip and tell her she has chubby cheeks
as we try to teach her about how it hurts to be made of gold,
even though it is the softest metal, and what does metal matter anyway,
when eventually bones become such a very fine dust.

Mice

I used to think about dying and feel
ok because I had you. I know
that's stupid, we wouldn't die
curled together and at the same
moment even if we lasted. Remember
the time the firemen tore up
my floorboards and found
those dead mice? I guess that's how
I always imagined us. Our tails
curling to perfect spirals, the
vertebrae of them aligned like bricks
in some modern but well-built
structure. Shell shaped.
The Fibonacci spiral. Perfection
in nature. It took me so long
after I left you, so many sleepless nights
staring at damp ceilings and trying not to think
about death, or about your bottom lip,
your nose, or your hands;
the way they tensed just before
sleep and held parts of me,
to remember that you and I
have never had tails.

Check Up

1. A proper poet told me once that all poems have a body.

2. This is a problem because I already have one body and it feels like too much. There are so many rules to remember for a body, for example:
The body must be fed, but not fed excessively and only certain kinds of foods. Sometimes it feels better not to feed the body, but this should be ignored.
The body must be kept clean.
The body must be kept out of strong sunlight.
The body must be dressed almost every single day, in ways sympathetic to social convention and the manner in which other people inside other bodies may be offended or aroused, and also in ways mindful of the weather and of the fashions of the time.
Largely, the body must be kept dry.
The body must retain an internal temperature of around 37 degrees Celsius.
From time to time, the body must be touched. This means many things and all of them are complicated.

3. I used to think poems were something over which I should have control. I make and remake a poem and if it's wrong I can change it or discard it. I can adjust the line breaks or remove cliche. A poem's shape is up to me, and a poem's name is up to me. A poem cannot want,
cannot itch,
cannot fall
apart.

4. Of course it is a metaphor, the poem/body thing. What it means is that poems contain breath. They contain space and their shape must hold for them to remain alive, to remain poems. But all bodies contain breath and all of them must hold their shape. All bod-

ies are metaphors. Signifiers. Bags of unseen stuff; that is, my body is made of bones and skin and meat and offal, and it is made of space. It is made of all the bees and blossoms and new-turned earth, all the stink bugs and dry rot and tiny curled mouse skeletons which fill its emptiness. None of this is up to me.

5. I tried for a while to keep my metaphor in check, but soon the doctor told me I must eat and I must put on clothes almost every day because he could see that I was skin and bones and he should be able to see neither. I pointed to my chest and said, *Do you know what's going on in here?* And he touched my body with his cold, medical hands, which is not one of the ways in which a body likes to be touched, and yet – his rubberised fingers in the gaps between my ribs; the coin of the stethoscope pressed against my skin. I said, *Can you hear?*

And I wanted him to say, Yes, I hear cherry blossoms falling onto wet grass ,
I hear love poems read to you by a man who gets up twice in the night for a cigarette and the sound of a refrigerator dispensing ice
I wanted him, even, to say,
Yes, I hear the scratching of rats at your sternum, that baby bird you saw fall and die one time, I hear its final squeak when you
breathe in. I hear everything that has ever been said about this body you wear every thought there has been about this body you travel in every single thing you have done for your to your body
And then I wanted him to say,
I hear what's inside, and it's ok, I can keep my ear here a while; rest my fingers in these perfect human grooves.

But he said none of that.

He said, *Your heartbeat, it's a little fast,*

I imagine it's anaemia

you really must try harder
to get three square meals a day, maybe more red meat – and he snapped

off the gloves, turned away, told me to hop down
from the examination table.

He drew the curtain so I could dress and

for a moment I hoped I might float away, like a tiny bird

heartbeat sharp as a new knife

chest aglow with bright flight

but my rubber soles hit rubber tile and I stood.

Today, I want to marry you.

The wedding would be intimate; as in, we'd make out at the altar
and your hand would be up my slip, the minister averting his eyes as he tried
to remember our middle names. And I think even if the marriage went to shit
quick our divorce would be hot too, or at least sad. I read a Donald Hall essay
on solitude last week, and he made marriage sound beautiful, and yesterday I turned
28, and the thrum of routine is beginning to be what I want, at least half the time.
Or maybe it's just that you make bad art with such earnest, and taught me to drive
with a bottle of champagne between your knees, and we hate all the same things,
and I think I'm in some shitty indie romcom or a radio-ready country song
with Levi cut-offs and warm bud lights and the other day, while I was being paid
to watch kids play with toy guns, I touched my lip and thought of yours;
text you something about drinking your cum and you touched yourself
too, and thought of me, and then we talked about what I should pick up
from the grocery store, and later we watched *Wings of Desire*
because I'd never seen it and it gave me an idea for a poem about a different
piece of art, and you cried when Damiel fell to the streets of Berlin
and saw in colour for the first time. And screw Berlin, I would sit in the back
of your truck with my ass cheeks out on burning metal for you, legs open, waiting
for fall leaves. I swear, I don't believe in marriage, but I don't believe in ghosts
and they still scare me. At the weekend you told me you heard one
in my apartment, and every night since I've woken and reached out for you.
I fucking swear, today I'd take your last name. I would promise to sleep
forever on top of the heavy pistol that I asked you to take the hell out
from beneath your mattress, where it always hummed in the dark.

Champs bar and cafe on a Tuesday night, and all the rest

Seven PM on a Tuesday, glowing cherries bob
by the bar where there's $1.50 Pabst, 50 cent wings,
and whole packs of Camels sucked down. This is tobacco country,
so we can't see for smoke. The TVs are warm and lonely
and the PBR is warm and popular, and my arms
are burned all over with perfect little circles.
One of them cooked right down to white fat, turned it
black edged. That will stay. This is coal country.
Men round here used to die properly,
from whatever mines do to you. Now this;
making the best of cigarette smoke and TVs,
counting breaths in and out and counting sets of college kids
passing through on longer journeys and counting dollar-fifties
and counting touchdowns, warm and lonely and knowing
every barman in town by name but through a vale and
grown sons across the street, shooting perfect games
of darts while chewing on fentanyl patches. This
is opioid country. The other day a deer leapt in front
of my car outside Kroger on a four lane highway
and we both stopped, trembling flesh, and we looked
at one another like *Woah* and then it turned and moved on.
Quick as a flash it was behind the big box store and I was
along 460 where there's barns all TRUMP 2020
and there's the cowboy store with the bolting horse bolted down,
the 30 foot cross made from white siding, and the long straight dip
that glimmers all summer with what isn't there. This
is Jesus country. I take my eyes from the road
and sure I see god, see ridgelines like sleeping legs, skies
like open mouths, see the mist settle over the mountains
like a wing, and below that it's all blue as cigarette smoke.

All our sexts as necessary fictions

There are tiny baby spiders in the corner of the ceiling.
You said once, and even in the moment this was too sweet
for either of us, *I want us to fuck and leave marks,*
so that we know when we're apart that we are alive
and we were together and it was beautiful. I had written
something similar recently; Bite marks
as flowers, fading to brown. In the poem it meant connection
and memory, and for a moment a dirty text
can feel like all that and love even though
what really lives there is lust, hard in Helvetica
Neue, even cleaner than the original Helvetica,
an update for the iPhone 4 and every model
since. I might say *I miss you next to me* or,
I woke up and for a second,
I thought you were beside me,
but I never know if I believe what I am writing,
or if I believe anything I read. I don't have the heart
to kill the baby spiders, but I bought
a venus fly trap and thought maybe
it would get confused and do it for me.
It's hard to trust anything that strikes me as beautiful
or profound. Am I just admiring someone else's way
with words? Am I jealous I didn't come up with that line?
Am I just enjoying being wanted?
Either way I much prefer, *I want to hold you down*
and pull your hair, to the stuff about
being alive and it being good and blah blah.
Maybe this is because being alive
is mostly falling into potholes, though
don't get me wrong, I like pizza
and sex, music, poems, fresh sheets, bodies of water,
a cigarette after a run, the smell of my dog, etc.
Once I fell into a pothole and found myself
in water up to my waist. I tell myself that fucking
is as beautiful and as boring as anything else,
but it's hard to believe. I want to stay right here.
I don't want to have a conversation. I don't want to haul
myself out of oily water and walk home heavy.
I want to feel you getting hard against my ass as we spoon.
I want to feel you getting hard against my ass as we spoon.
I want to print out all our dirty texts and pry open my body
like a tin can, bend back my ribs, and stuff myself full

of them, even if my hands are sliced open. I want to paper my walls
with them. I tried to repot the venus flytrap. Give it room
to spread its roots and grow, but I think I overwatered it
and then it died, sunk into itself like it was in mourning.
I can't throw the body away. The baby spiders are beginning
to migrate from the corner of the ceiling. You send me a picture,
and through the cracked screen of my phone
it doesn't even look like any part of a person.

A poem for my IUD

My partner is afraid of the dog pissing
on graves and I wouldn't want to teach
that sort of superstition to a child. Many of the graves
are old and tree-eaten and by any metric the bones
beneath them are forgotten. Is it a quiet radical act
when I return to the sexual health clinic, yes, 30 now,
and say *Stick another one in there will you*. Last time
which yes was five years ago believe it
or not this was me the same creature
but so different - the nurse said *Oh good
twenty-five, when it comes out you'll be
ready to think about children*. Sure
I think about them often, wipe snot and things
for money wonder about their teeth and how
small they are, the teeth, sitting unknowing
straight and white and soon they will be pushed
rudely out by the *real* teeth which will do
the grownup biting. When I was 22 I tried
for the first to to get an intrauterine device
inserted and that visit the doctor said
after bumping up against my little cervix,
tiny locked door, *Come back when you've
had a baby*. Please get this straight,
when you ask me to tick boxes on your forms
I will sure, but looking inside me doesn't mean
you know me at all. I am afraid as anything of
the seeds in a pomegranate and of weird bug
holes in leaves where larvae have chomped
and after the inserted IUD I bled for weeks and
weeks a bit, and it hurt like a fist
holding itself soso tight below my belly-
button and into my back and thighs and I had
a cold the first time I fucked after too so stuff was coming
from everywhere! What has my IUD seen me through -
many strangers, the two French men, the girl with
the cowboy boots who I met at a cheese counter,
three countries. That's liberation, baby! Yes! In Tennessee
I posed in front of a doorway like a shark's sharpsharpsharp
mouth with my girlfriend and inside there were loads
of dead hermit crabs and WHEN THEY COME
FOR OUR GUNS WE'LL GIVE EM OUR BULLETS

and we were so far from the sea of course the hermit
crabs were dead, and they have no teeth. It isn't about
what I want or don't want, more about having to bite
so much! Honestly, I don't even know what I'm biting.
Have you ever seen pelicans diving
down to the shallows to eat at sunset, big beaks
happyopen, dodging small docked boats?
They do it every single evening, yeh, every evening
filling up on microplastics! I watched three times, it was cool,
but then I got food poisoning. I've got all my real teeth,
with fillings added too, and I have ¾ wisdom and god the world
is beautiful, isn't it beautiful? Look at it!
Don't you want to kick it in the mouth?

Cat

There was this cat, with one ear missing and a hole
right to its brain. I had never seen a brain like that
before, in a head cracked open. I've seen them in jars
and at meat markets, covered in flies sometimes and blood
everywhere across tiles designed to show it
off, but I'd never seen a brain still in use.
We said nothing as we walked past. The cat
meowed. The cat went about its business and we
went about ours. We were on holiday. The cat cleaned its one ear.
There was a breeze block nearby. We didn't have to say, *should we*.
We knew we wouldn't. It was minutes later, on another street
you said, *maybe we should have put it out its misery*. I said
It wasn't in misery. You said, *It will be, though*.
We went to find dinner, and then the sea.

Living through history

I change the water my cutting is floating in, rub
its stem clean, careful of the new-teeth root buds
pushing out for for life. I try rye flour with my starter
which has been breathing for years and bubbles away
quite blind in the cupboard. I am on the phone to the credit
card people and the debt collection people and they are working
from home so can't actually take bank details right now.
Though I am staying out of bed, I dream of an airport
pint. A pint on the way between a place and another place,
a pint I can't afford. Lying to a stranger with a wedding ring
about my name and what I do, Ofsted inspector, hairdresser,
double glazing sales. The dog shits on someone's lawn
and I can't find a bag. The cutting is doing a slow kind of well.
Cuttings exist in cutting time. Sometimes nothing for days
or weeks. My final wisdom tooth Is pushing through and I am
almost 30. We eat box mac and cheese from a mixing bowl,
add too much butter. Longing is a liar and always has been.
The sunset from the windowsill is thin and iridescent as sea
shells. The sky is an embarrassed ear. There are no aeroplanes,
not even trails of white where they used to be.

South for Winter

When I imagine myself rotting it isn't mourning it's a mantra. A lesson in living and letting go. I wonder where roots will grow and what bones they will grasp and snap. Driving through the south the roads are so wide and quiet they draw my attention. After looking for so long at a lack, the overpasses tangled in the sky are striking. Outside Vicksburg, Miss, I see a chunk of one naked and on its side. Its huge steel beams jutt like the ribs of a beast in an oversized elephant graveyard. Everything this far south makes me think of mourning. Not just the swamps and the air like breathing into a palm and the slow way people talk and the bugs; even the welcome centre where we park to sleep seems to be a temporary thing. The attempt at Old South opulence inside is wailing and wailing: there's gilded horses bearing their teeth and too much carpeting in the squat building. I blink and see the place moth eaten. The mounted heads of beasts eaten up, the horses on their sides. Coyotes are curled on the sofas, avoiding the springs that have broken through. They stalk the sidewalk where the guard told me *no dogs, dogs on the grass only*. The motor vehicles that are left are rusted and home to snakes. This is a place that wants to return to before us. This is a place that wants to be let go, a place that imagines itself rotting and it isn't a mantra, it's a plea.

Acknowledgements

Thank you to the journals where these poems originally appeared:

The Moth Magazine, 'The First Time They Want You', 'Living Through History'
Spam, 'A Memory' and 'Last Summers'
Hobart, 'Religious Art', 'A Diaristic Quality but Everything is Still Gone' and 'Jonas Mekas at the Tate Modern'
Lighthouse, 'Bed Stuy you can't ever have me'
Crabfat Magazine, 'All our sexts as necessary fictions'
The Babel Tower Noticeboard, 'Check Up'
Copper Nickel, 'Cat'
Crested Tit Rewilding Anthology, 'South for Winter'
The Cardiff Review, 'There have been many times food has been like...'
Fruit, 'Poem for my IUD'

LAY OUT YOUR UNREST

www.ingramcontent.com/pod-product-compliance
Lightning Source LLC
Chambersburg PA
CBHW061348040426
42444CB00011B/3147